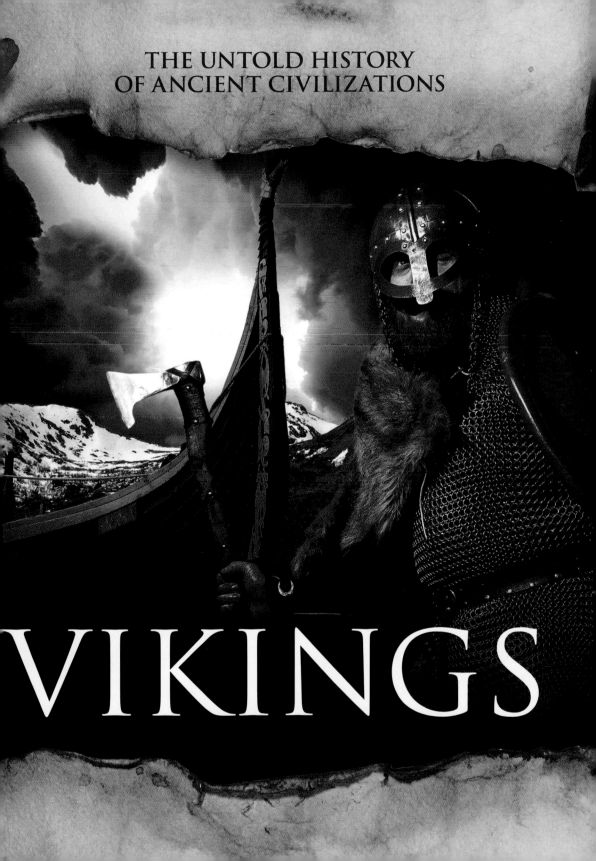

THE UNTOLD HISTORY
OF ANCIENT CIVILIZATIONS

VIKINGS

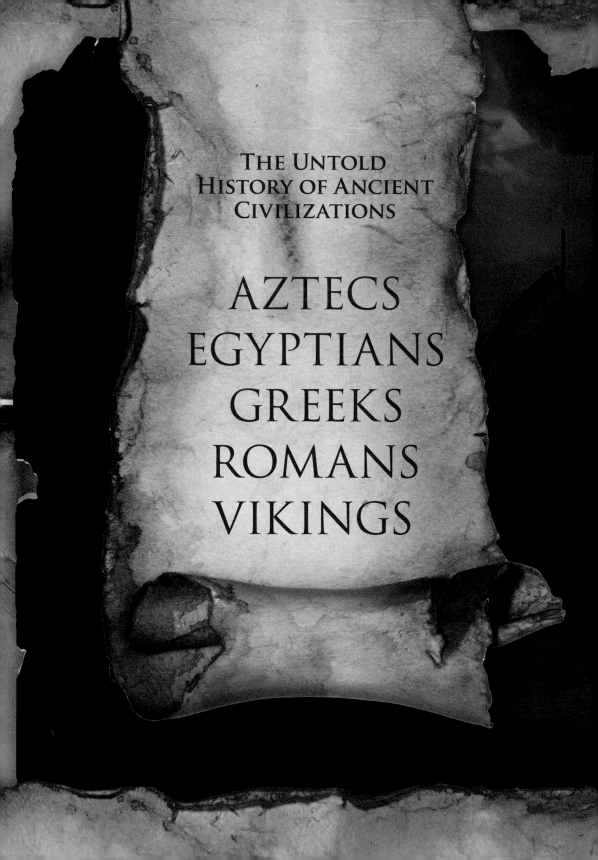

THE UNTOLD HISTORY OF ANCIENT CIVILIZATIONS

AZTECS
EGYPTIANS
GREEKS
ROMANS
VIKINGS

THE UNTOLD HISTORY
OF ANCIENT CIVILIZATIONS

VIKINGS

MASON CREST
PHILADELPHIA
MIAMI

Mason Crest
450 Parkway Drive, Suite D
Broomall, Pennsylvania 19008
(866) MCP-BOOK (toll-free)
www.masoncrest.com

ISBN (hardback) 978-1-4222-3522-5
ISBN (series) 978-1-4222-3517-1
ISBN (ebook) 978-1-4222-8342-4

Cataloging-in-Publication Data on file with the Library of Congress

Developed and produced by Mason Crest
Editor: Keri DeDeo
Interior and cover design: Jana Rade
Production: Michelle Luke

QR CODES AND LINKS TO THIRD-PARTY CONTENT

CONTENTS

KEY ICONS TO LOOK FOR:

 WORDS TO UNDERSTAND: These words with their easy-to-understand definitions will increase the reader's understanding of the text while building vocabulary skills.

 SIDEBARS: This boxed material within the main text allows readers to build knowledge, gain insights, explore possibilities, and broaden their perspectives by weaving together additional information to provide realistic and holistic perspectives.

 EDUCATIONAL VIDEOS: Readers can view videos by scanning our QR codes, providing them with additional educational content to supplement the text. Examples include news coverage, moments in history, speeches, iconic sports moments, and much more!

 TEXT-DEPENDENT QUESTIONS: These questions send the reader back to the text for more careful attention to the evidence presented there.

 RESEARCH PROJECTS: Readers are pointed toward areas of further inquiry connected to each chapter. Suggestions are provided for projects that encourage deeper research and analysis.

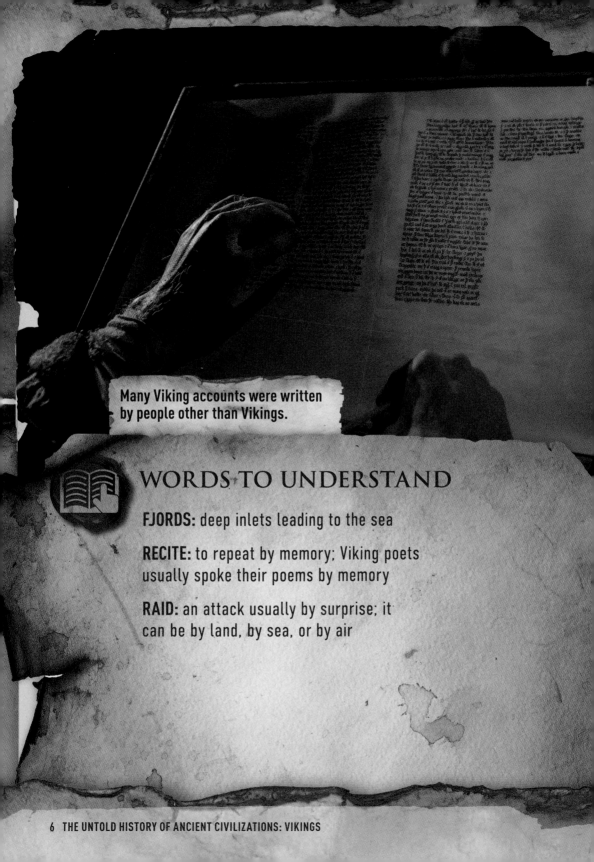

Many Viking accounts were written by people other than Vikings.

WORDS TO UNDERSTAND

FJORDS: deep inlets leading to the sea

RECITE: to repeat by memory; Viking poets usually spoke their poems by memory

RAID: an attack usually by surprise; it can be by land, by sea, or by air

CHAPTER 1

OH NO, HERE COME THE VIKINGS

T horstein Cod-Biter, Ulf the Unwashed, Einar Belly-Shaker, Aud the Deep-Minded—no, these aren't comic book characters. These are real people who lived more than 1,000 years ago in Norway, Denmark, and Sweden. And if you saw them coming your way, you wouldn't be laughing.

Today, we call the people of these northern lands "Vikings," a word that probably once meant **raider**. Many people still think of Vikings as simply fierce invaders, but there was much more to them than that. They were also farmers, explorers, traders, and skilled craftspeople.

The age of the Vikings lasted from about AD 780 to 1100. In that time, they left their homelands in

Explore the Vikings' world in this video from the National Museum of Denmark.

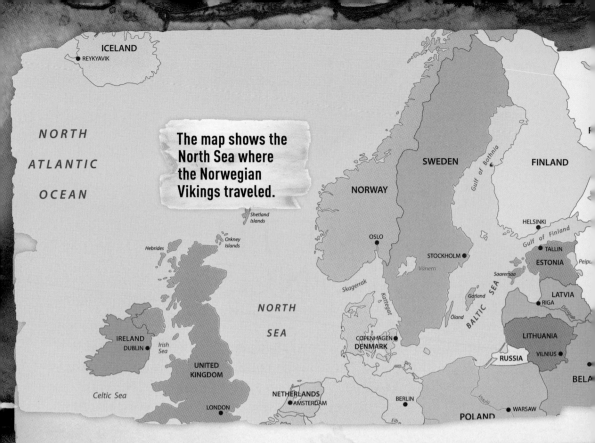

The map shows the North Sea where the Norwegian Vikings traveled.

modern-day Norway, Denmark, and Sweden and set off on great journeys in all directions.

Norwegian Vikings were looking for lands to settle and sailed west across the Atlantic. Danes and Norwegians crossed the North Sea to raid and invade the rich lands of Britain, Ireland, France, and Germany. Meanwhile, Swedish Vikings traveled east and south, along the rivers of Russia, on trading journeys. In their homelands, such as Norway, the Vikings usually lived close to water, along **fjords**.

NICKNAMES

Vikings did not write books. So, much of what we know about them comes from accounts written by the people whose lands they raided. Instead, Vikings loved to tell stories and **recite** poems. In the thirteenth and fourteenth centuries, these were finally written down in books called sagas. It is from the sagas that we know that the Vikings were jokers who liked giving each other strange nicknames. For example, a big, strong, powerful man named Thorbjorn was called Thorbjorn the Feeble.

Use this rune alphabet to write your name and other words.

| FEHU | URUZ | THURISAZ | ANSUZ | RAIDHO | KAUNAZ | GEBO | WUNJI |

| HAGALAZ | NAUDIZ | ISA | JARA | EIHWAZ | PERTHU | ALGIZ | SOWULC |

| TEIWAZ | BERKANA | EHWAZ | MANNAZ | LAGUZ | INGWAZ | DAGAZ | OTHAL |

TEXT-DEPENDENT QUESTIONS

1. How do we know so much about the Vikings?
2. When was the age of the Vikings?
3. Where did the Vikings go?

RESEARCH PROJECT

The Vikings didn't write books, but they did write...mostly on rocks. Use the image of the runic alphabet above, and write your name. What other words can you write using the runic alphabet?

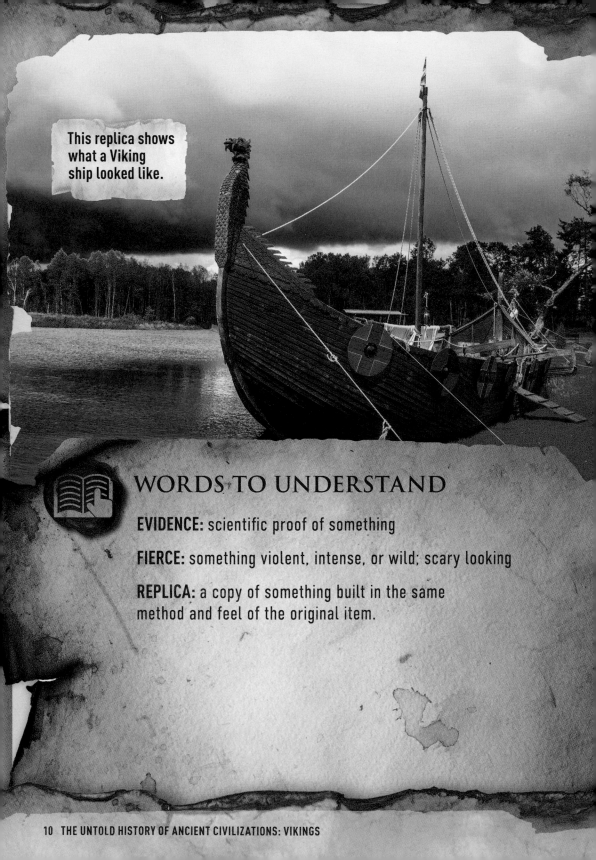

This replica shows what a Viking ship looked like.

WORDS TO UNDERSTAND

EVIDENCE: scientific proof of something

FIERCE: something violent, intense, or wild; scary looking

REPLICA: a copy of something built in the same method and feel of the original item.

CHAPTER 2

SHIPS AHOY

One of the things people think about that go with Vikings is their warships. But Vikings also built beautiful boats and ships in which they buried their dead. Scientists still aren't sure what this meant to them. Perhaps the Vikings thought of death as the start of a journey to another world—and Vikings traveled by ship. Thanks to this custom, we can still see ships built by the Vikings today.

The Gokstad ship was a *langskip*, or longship, a narrow, slim warship built for speed. It was strong enough to cross stormy seas but light enough to travel up shallow rivers or be dragged up onto a beach. With ships like this, Vikings could get almost anywhere.

Vikings loved their ships and gave them names. One of the most famous was Olaf Tryggvason's Long Serpent and Erik, the Earl of Lade's Ironbard. The *prows* (fronts) were decorated with the carved heads of snakes, dragons, or

THE GOKSTAD SHIP

The best-preserved Viking ship burial was found in 1881 at Gokstad in Norway. The ship, 70 feet (23.3 m) long, was built of overlapping oak planks. When the ship was found, it had sixty-four shields, so scientists believe the ship carried at least that many crew. A **replica** of the ship, built in 1893, sailed from Norway to Canada in twenty-eight days.

This 3-D illustration provides a sense of what a Viking invasion must have looked like.

Can you imagine a ship with such a carving coming at you? How would you feel?

other dangerous animals. To a Viking warrior, sailing into battle might have felt like riding on the back of a **fierce** dragon. To the people who saw them coming, it was terrifying.

Although the Gokstad ship looks plain today, it may once have been brightly colored. There is **evidence** for this on the wall hanging called the Bayeux Tapestry, which shows longships painted in colored stripes with patterned sails.

The Bayeux Tapestry shows the Norman invasion of England in the eleventh century and Viking longboats.

TEXT-DEPENDENT QUESTIONS

1. Other than warships, what other reason did the Vikings build ships?
2. Why are Viking warships called "longships"?
3. How do scientists know that the Viking ships were likely brightly colored?

RESEARCH PROJECT

There are multiple websites and videos on the Internet that explain how to make a Viking longship out of cardboard. For example, the We and Us Ltd site (http://www.weandus.ie/how_to_make.html) provides PDF instructions and a template for making a longship from a cereal box. Make sure to click on the image of the Viking ship.

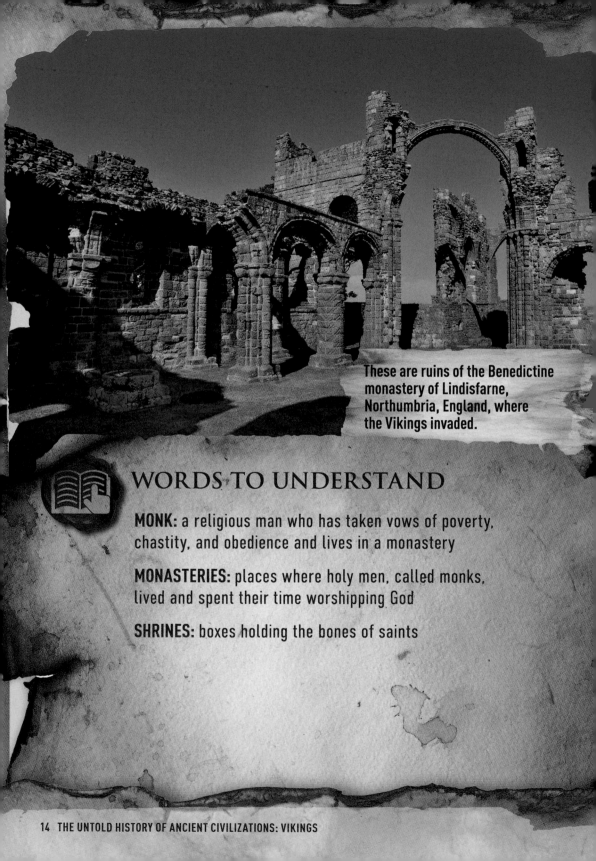

These are ruins of the Benedictine monastery of Lindisfarne, Northumbria, England, where the Vikings invaded.

WORDS TO UNDERSTAND

MONK: a religious man who has taken vows of poverty, chastity, and obedience and lives in a monastery

MONASTERIES: places where holy men, called monks, lived and spent their time worshipping God

SHRINES: boxes holding the bones of saints

CHAPTER 3

SURPRISE ATTACK

Picture a sea coast with waves crashing to shore. Along the way, in Britain and Ireland, are **monasteries** built by monks looking for solitude, serenity, and safety. These Christian holy men spent their days worshipping God, never guessing what—or who—was about to show up. The last thing they expected was to be attacked by strange men in longships.

The first and most shocking raid on a monastery took place in the year AD 793. The monastery of Lindisfarne, one of the holiest places in Britain, was attacked. Some of the **monks** were killed, while others were taken away to be slaves. The Vikings took everything but a Bible and the coffin of a saint.

From a Viking point of view, Lindisfarne was a perfect place to attack. It was right next to the sea, it had beaches to make landing boats easy, and the monks who lived there were holy men who did not have weapons or know how to fight back. They also had many treasures, such as gold-decorated Bibles and jeweled **shrines**.

MAKING FRIENDS THE VIKING WAY

Viking warriors looked up to people who were generous and would follow only leaders who regularly gave away their wealth. Such chieftains and kings were called "ring givers." This meant that to win power and keep his men's loyalty, a Viking leader needed a constant supply of wealth. This was a good reason to keep raiding Britain and Ireland.

This Viking hoard, buried about AD 905 in Lancashire England, is the largest ever found in Western Europe.

Raids did not always go according to plan. A year after Lindisfarne was attacked, a fleet of Viking longships raided the nearby monastery at Jarrow. Before they could sail home, their fleet was hit by a violent storm. Some of the longships sank, and many men drowned. The survivors who swam ashore were killed by the angry English.

A gold Bible such as this one would have been a large treasure for the Vikings.

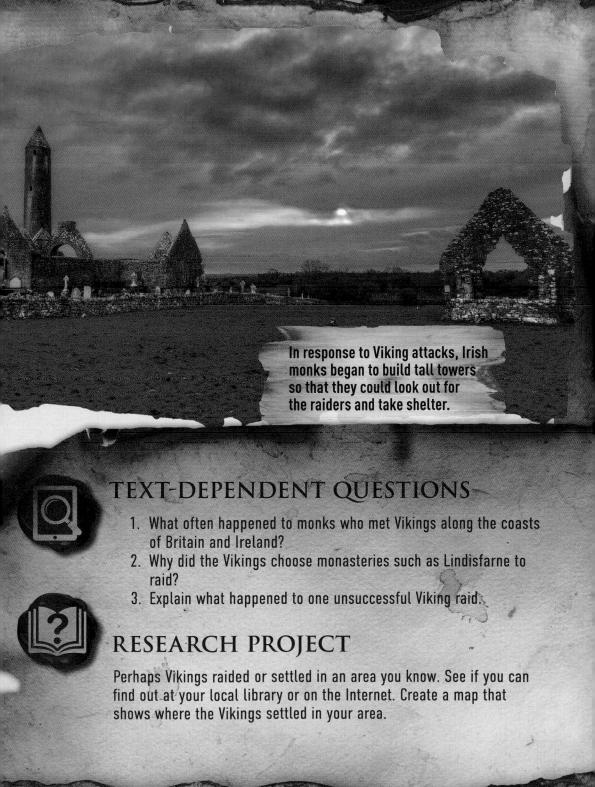

In response to Viking attacks, Irish monks began to build tall towers so that they could look out for the raiders and take shelter.

TEXT-DEPENDENT QUESTIONS

1. What often happened to monks who met Vikings along the coasts of Britain and Ireland?
2. Why did the Vikings choose monasteries such as Lindisfarne to raid?
3. Explain what happened to one unsuccessful Viking raid.

RESEARCH PROJECT

Perhaps Vikings raided or settled in an area you know. See if you can find out at your local library or on the Internet. Create a map that shows where the Vikings settled in your area.

The Vikings knew that England was a land of great wealth. Unlike early Viking rulers, English kings minted their own silver coins.

WORDS TO UNDERSTAND

AGONIZE: to be in great pain and suffering

AVENGE: to cause harm to someone out of a sense of wrongly placed justice

ENTERTAINMENT: something done for fun

CHAPTER 4

THE TRUTH IN THE TALE

Once upon a time, according to the Viking sagas, there was a man name Ragnar Hairy-Breeches.

The poor man was captured by the English king, Aella of York. Aella threw Ragnar into a pit filled with poisonous snakes, where he died a slow, **agonizing** death.

Back in Denmark, Ragnar had a son, Ivar the Boneless. Ivar decided to **avenge** his father's death. He raised a great army and invaded England. Ivar captured and killed Aella.

The story of Ivar was written long after it took place, and most of it was probably made up for **entertainment**, like stories of Robin Hood. Yet there was a Viking called Ivar. He was one of the leaders of the Great Army of Danes, which invaded England in the year AD 865. Aella of York was killed by these Vikings.

Warfare experts talk about armor and gear worn by ancient Vikings.

North Sea

Sylt

Can you spot the Rhine River in Germany?

ENMANY

Hamburg

Bremen

THERLANDS

Hanover

BERLIN

Elbe

Dusseldorf

Leipzig

Cologne

Dresden

ELGIUM

Rhine

GERMANY

Frankfurt

Koblenz

Wiesbaden

CZECH R

Mainz

Heidelberg

Danube

Baden-Baden

Stuttgart

FRANCE

Freudenstadt

Freiberg

Munich

AUS

SWITZERLAND

King Alfred the Great brought peace between the Vikings and the English.

As time went on, the Vikings got more organized, and they were able to launch the Great Army. For years, wealth from raiding trips had been pouring into the Viking homelands. More and more men wanted their share of the treasure. By the 850s, Viking fleets of hundreds of ships were setting off across the North Sea. They sailed up rivers, such as the Rhine in Germany and the Seine in France, to attack big towns.

SMELLY BELLY

When a Viking was wounded in the belly, he was given a meal of oatmeal porridge flavored with onions. If his wound smelled of onions, it meant that his guts had been pierced, and he would probably die. But if there was no smell, it meant that he might well recover, so his wounds would be bandaged.

RESEARCH PROJECT

MAKE A VIKING SHIELD

YOU WILL NEED:
- Acrylic paint (red was a popular color for the Vikings)
- Silver duct tape
- Colored paper
- Tacky glue
- Old cardboard box
- Old egg carton
- Colored pens
- Pencil
- Scissors
- Clear tape

INSTRUCTIONS:
Top Tip! An old cardboard box is ideal for this—you don't want the cardboard to be too thin.

1. Find something round to draw around, like a large plate or mixing bowl, and place it on your cardboard box.
2. Draw around it and cut it out.
3. Mark out the four sections of your shield by drawing a vertical line down the middle and a horizontal line across.
4. Paint two opposite corners of your shield with the paint.
5. While the paint is drying, take your egg carton and cut out one of the raised sections—this will form the center 3-D part of your shield.
6. Cover it in silver duct tape.
7. Stick duct tape along the center lines of your shield so it divides it into four sections.
8. Then stick duct tape around the edge. You will need to cut lots of smaller lengths of tape and overlap them as you go around the shield.
9. With the glue, stick your egg box piece onto the center of your shield.
   Top Tip! When sticking your centerpiece down, hold it for a few minutes to help it stick.
10. Choose some colored paper and cut out four small circles. Draw a little spot in the middle of each with your pen. Stick the circles on each joint around the edge of the shield.
11. Now you need to make a handle for your shield. Cut a strip of cardboard and using tape, secure it to the back.

Adapted from blog.hobbycraft.co.uk

The Vikings in the Great Army were not raiders. They were conquerors. They spent fourteen years moving around England, fighting and beating one king after another. Eventually, in AD 878, they made peace with the last English king, Alfred the Great. The English and the Vikings shared the land between them.

Use this photo of a Viking shield as a model for your own shield.

TEXT-DEPENDENT QUESTIONS

1. Why was a dying Viking warrior given porridge with onions in it?
2. How did the Vikings travel to large cities?
3. Who was Alfred the Great?

KALSOY KUNOY VIDHOY

EYSTUROY Gjógv

FUGLOY

Trøllanes

Mikladalur

Kirkja

STREYMOY

SVÍNOY

Leirvík

Syðrugøta

BORDHOY

Slættanes

MYKINES

ATLANTIC OCEAN

Rituvík

Nes Æðuvík

Kaldbak

Hvítanes

VÁGAR

Norðradalur

Syðradalur

Tórshavn

NOLSOY

Koltur

Velbastaður

Hestur Kirkjubøur

HESTUR Hælur

FAROE

ISLANDS

Skopun

SANDOY

Skálavík

Húsavík

Skarvanes Dalur

Skúvoy

These are the Faroe
Islands—one place where
the Vikings explored.

WORDS TO UNDERSTAND

ARCHAEOLOGIST: someone who digs up remains from
earlier times to find out what life was like in the past

COURAGE: when someone faces danger despite being afraid

TURF HOUSE: a house built with a grass roof; the grass
kept the house cool in summer and warm in winter

CHAPTER 5

ACCIDENTAL EXPLORERS

Sailing across the North Sea takes **courage**, but sailing across the North Atlantic Ocean is another story entirely. These brave Viking explorers were looking for new lands. They reached, and named, the Faroe Islands, Iceland, and Greenland. From Greenland, they sailed on to North America, which they called Vinland (Wine Land). Scientists have found evidence that the Vikings reached North America as early as AD 1000, hundreds of years before any European explorer.

In Iceland people wrote down Viking adventures in the sagas. According to them, Iceland, Greenland, and North America were all found by accident by Vikings blown off course on voyages to other places. When they got home and described their discoveries, others decided to follow in their footsteps.

CRYSTAL GAZING

In the Viking's time compasses had not yet been invented. Instead, they found their way at sea by the height of the Sun, which told them how far to the north or south they were. On cloudy days, when the Sun was hidden, the sagas say they used a crystal called a "Sun stone." They held this crystal up, moving it until the light seen through it changed color. This showed the location of the sun.

RESEARCH PROJECT

GROW YOUR OWN TURF

YOU WILL NEED:
- Disposable cup
- Paint (acrylic paint is best for this project)
- Paintbrush
- Marker
- Dirt
- Grass seed
- Optional: wiggly eyes

* Note: Acrylic paint is not washable, so young children should wear old clothes and do their work away from carpet and other household fabrics. If you catch the paint while it's wet, you can usually get it out, but it dries very quickly, so you have to be fast.

INSTRUCTIONS:
1. Buy grass seed.
2. Paint the outside front half of the cup with whatever color you want or use a colored cup.
3. Glue wiggly eyes or draw eyes onto the painted side of the cup and draw a mouth as well. This makes a face for your grass seed cup. You could even draw a house so you're making a house with grass on top!
4. Plant the grass seed. Make sure you do this on newspaper or outside.
5. Fill the cup with dirt about ½ inch (1.27 cm) from the top.
6. Sprinkle the grass seed over the dirt in the cup.
7. Sprinkle more dirt over the grass seed.
8. Now wait and watch your grass grow!
9. Water the grass every day. Don't overwater the grass.
10. Once your grass starts getting really long, you can give it a "haircut" with scissors so that it will start growing more again. This is also a messy process, so do it outside or place newspaper under the area where you are cutting it.

In the 860s, a man called Floki Raven set out to find Iceland. Floki earned his nickname because he took ravens with him on his voyage. Birds in the air can see farther than men on a ship. Floki knew that his birds would spot land before he did. So, he released the birds, and when they did not see land, they flew back to his ship. When at last they saw land, they flew off. And Floki sailed after them. Floki didn't care for Iceland, however, and left, never to return.

Until recently, the only evidence that Vikings reached North America was in the sagas. However, in the 1960s, **archaeologists** discovered a group of Viking **turf houses** in Newfoundland, just off the coast of North America. Scientists now think this was a hunting camp used by the Vikings from time to time. This discovery proved that the sagas were telling the truth.

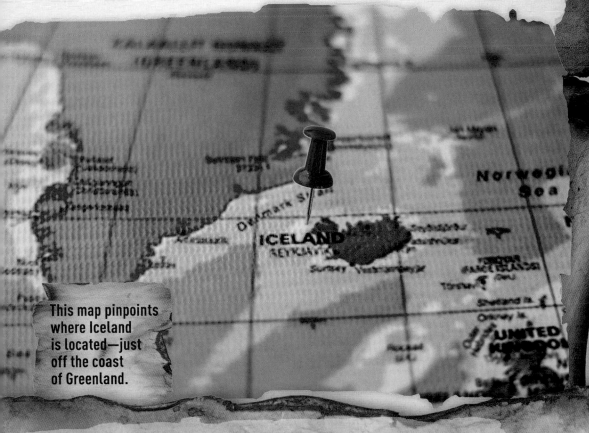

This map pinpoints where Iceland is located—just off the coast of Greenland.

This is a monument of Leif Eriksson in Newfoundland.

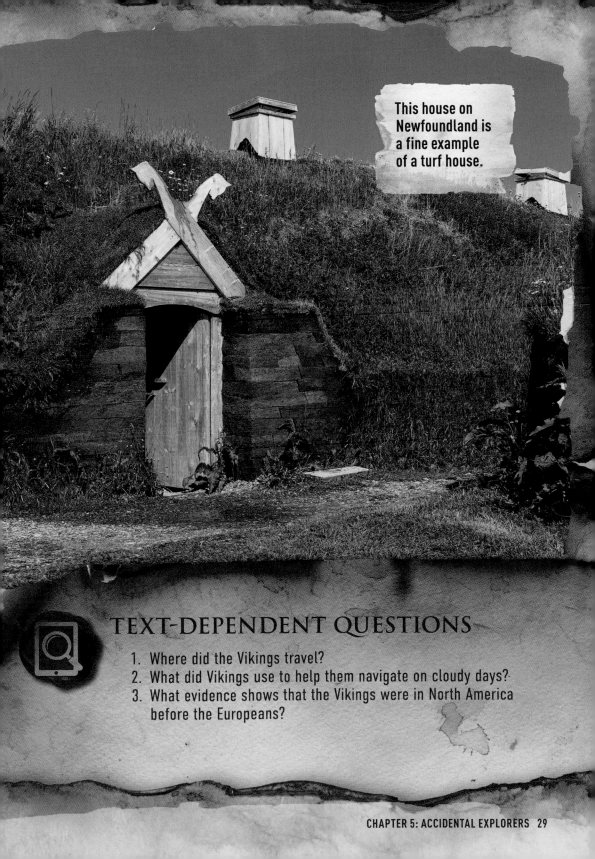

This house on Newfoundland is a fine example of a turf house.

TEXT-DEPENDENT QUESTIONS

1. Where did the Vikings travel?
2. What did Vikings use to help them navigate on cloudy days?
3. What evidence shows that the Vikings were in North America before the Europeans?

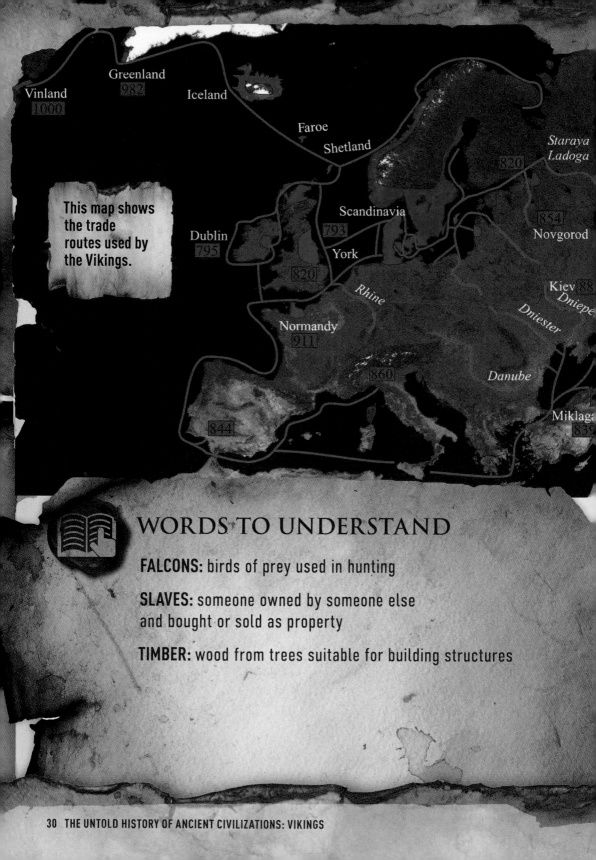

Vinland
1000

Greenland
982

Iceland

Faroe

Shetland

Staraya
Ladoga

820

This map shows
the trade
routes used by
the Vikings.

Scandinavia

793

Dublin
795

York

820

854

Novgorod

Rhine

Normandy
911

Kiev 88

Dniepe

Dniester

Danube

860

844

Miklaga

839

WORDS TO UNDERSTAND

FALCONS: birds of prey used in hunting

SLAVES: someone owned by someone else
and bought or sold as property

TIMBER: wood from trees suitable for building structures

CHAPTER 6

SHOW ME THE MONEY

L ike the Europeans that would follow them, Vikings were highly successful traders. What was their secret to success? They had the best ships and were willing to travel great distances as long as there was money in it. Viking traders did business with almost everyone, from Lapland in the icy North to Greece and the hot lands of the Arabs in the South.

Trade flourished because Vikings settled in many different places yet kept in touch with their homelands. Merchant ships from Norway made regular journeys across the sea to Iceland and Greenland, carrying **timber** to sell. They exchanged this for wool, furs, and wild **falcons**. They were careful businessmen. They carried scales to weigh coins to make sure they were getting a fair deal. Viking trade led to the growth of towns, such as Dublin and Limerick in Ireland, York in England, and Hedeby in Denmark.

VIKING CURRENCY

The Vikings didn't have currency. Instead, the Vikings used what they had for trade: fur, amber, iron, and walrus tusks. When they had it, the Viking merchants used silver valued by weight rather than by different types of coin.

Wild falcons like this one were used to help the Vikings hunt.

Viking traders would buy and sell anything, even people. Ireland was a big source of thralls, or **slaves**. These were British or Eastern European people captured by Vikings in raids. Many Irish men and women ended up as thralls, doing the hard work on farms in places like Iceland. In Iceland, a big, strong, male thrall was said to cost twenty-four cows. A woman, who was not as strong, cost just eight cows.

Many slaves were sold to farms like this in Iceland.

This money comes from Norway.

TEXT-DEPENDENT QUESTIONS

1. Why did the Vikings do so well as traders?
2. Where did the Vikings trade?
3. What were some of the items the Viking merchants used to trade?

RESEARCH PROJECT

Have you ever wondered what kind of money the Scandinavians use now? Most of the countries use fancy colored bills and gold- or silver-colored coin. They're not necessarily made out of gold or silver. What metals are used to make coins? Is it different from nation to nation? How is the worth measured of such coin? Do some Internet research to discover some of the answers to these questions. Create a photo collage of the different kinds of currency you discovered.

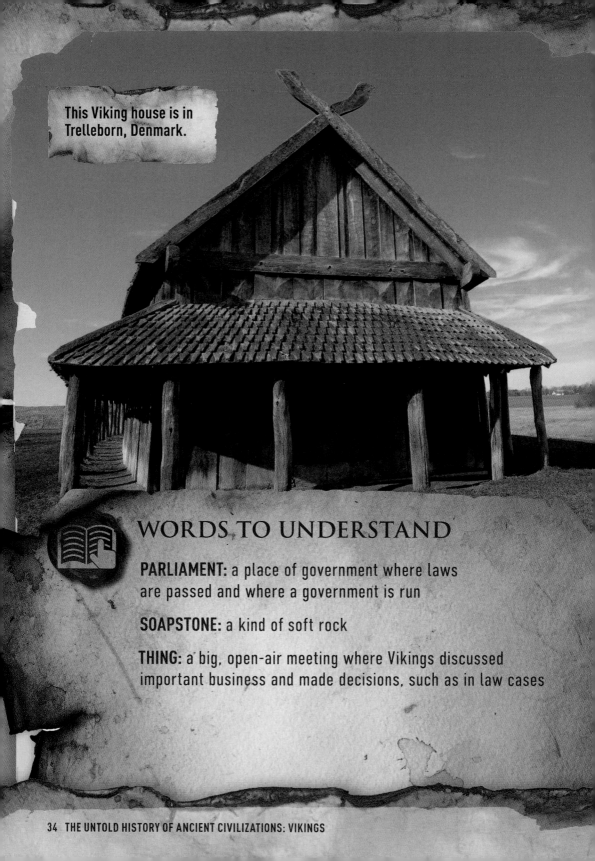

This Viking house is in Trelleborn, Denmark.

WORDS TO UNDERSTAND

PARLIAMENT: a place of government where laws are passed and where a government is run

SOAPSTONE: a kind of soft rock

THING: a big, open-air meeting where Vikings discussed important business and made decisions, such as in law cases

CHAPTER 7

HOME CROWDED HOME

Some kids share their bedrooms with a brother or sister. Can you imagine sharing your room not only with your brother or sister, but your mom and dad, your grandparents, and maybe a cousin or two? Vikings lived with many people all sharing one big room with a central fireplace for warmth, cooking, and light and benches around the walls. Houses like this were common in Viking times.

Viking families sat around the fire in the evenings and slept on the benches at night, wrapped up in furs and blankets. In the cold, northern lands, it was more important to keep warm than to have your own private bedroom.

Watch as this video shows turf buildings in Iceland and Newfoundland.

This modern reconstruction of a farm in Iceland shows the typical long and narrow shape of a Viking home.

In Sweden, Denmark, England, and Ireland, people lived in villages and towns. In Norway, the Scottish Isles, Iceland, and Greenland, they lived in single farmhouses, often miles (kilometers) from their nearest neighbor. The only time they might meet their neighbors was at a big, open-air meeting called a **thing**. The thing, which was held regularly, was a place

A SEABIRD TO SEE BY

Seabirds, such as gulls, have a lot of oil in their bodies. Vikings caught gulls and boiled them in a pot, collecting the oil that floated to the top of the water. They used this oil to light their homes, burning it in lamps carved from soft **soapstone.**

to do business, arrange marriages, sort out quarrels, and try legal cases. Some things still occur today. The Icelandic **parliament** is known as the Althing, the Norwegian parliament is called the Storting, and the Faroese parliament is the Løgting.

Thanks to archaeological remains, such as this longhouse found at Jarshof in Shetland, we know the shape of Viking houses.

This reconstruction in Newfoundland shows how cluttered with belongings a Viking home must have been.

TEXT-DEPENDENT QUESTIONS

1. Why did families sleep in one big room rather than have separate bedrooms?
2. What is a thing?
3. What are the Icelandic, Norwegian, and Faroese parliaments called?

RESEARCH PROJECT

Make Your Own Soap Carving

Although soap isn't exactly like soapstone, it is more easily accessible and easier to work with. For this project, you need a simple bar of soap, a plastic knife, and small cookies cutters.

Hint: Choose a soap that is easy to cut, carve, and rearrange. Do a short Internet search to find the best brand for such a use. You can then rub out the brand name if it has one.

- You can completely cut out the shape, carve the soap, or make a 3-D image on the soap.
- To make a 3-D carving just press the cookie cutter in. Then use your knife to cut out some of the soap surrounding the cookie cutter to make a nice flat surface.

You can carve your own designs in soap! Just use a plastic knife instead of a sharp one.

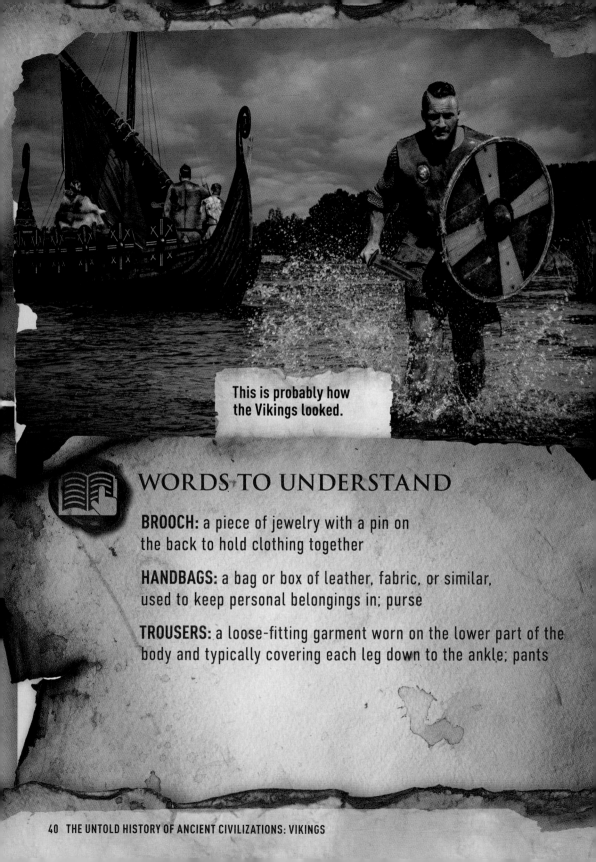

This is probably how the Vikings looked.

WORDS TO UNDERSTAND

BROOCH: a piece of jewelry with a pin on the back to hold clothing together

HANDBAGS: a bag or box of leather, fabric, or similar, used to keep personal belongings in; purse

TROUSERS: a loose-fitting garment worn on the lower part of the body and typically covering each leg down to the ankle; pants

CHAPTER 8

FLAIR FOR FASHION

When people think of Vikings, they imagine long, bushy beards, horned helmets, and maybe a little bit of a smell. But in fact, the opposite is true. Viking men and women cared a lot about their appearance and took great pains to look their best.

An English writer complained that Viking men were popular with Englishwomen because they changed their clothes, combed their hair, and had a bath on Saturdays—unlike Englishmen! Swedish Vikings even called Saturday "bath day."

Vikings certainly combed their hair. Combs made from animal bone are common finds from Viking sites. It might not have been about good looks. They likely wanted to get rid of fleas and head lice, which must have been common in Viking houses.

GRAVE CLUES

Most of what we know about Viking clothes comes from items found in graves. Cloth hardly ever lasts long in graves. So, archaeologists have to work out how people dressed from other clues, such as the position on a skeleton of metal brooches or buckles. Two large, oval brooches usually are found by the shoulders of female skeletons, showing us where these were worn.

The strangest clue about how Vikings looked comes from an Arab merchant called Al-Tartushi. He visited Hedeby in Denmark in about AD 950 and wrote that the men and women there wore eye makeup. "When they use it," he wrote, "'the beauty of both men and women increases."

Women wore long-sleeved linen or woolen tunics, which reached their ankles. On top, they had a woolen apron dress held in place by a pair of big, oval **brooches**. There was often a chain or string of beads between the brooches. Without **handbags** or pockets, this chain was a useful place to hang small items, such as keys, combs, or scissors.

These reconstructed wooden hair combs are based on findings in ancient Viking houses.

Viking graves such as these reveal important facts about how Vikings dressed.

Men wore **trousers**, short tunics, and a cloak fastened at one shoulder with a brooch. Swords, knives, and other belongings dangled from their leather belts. From carvings, we know that Viking men grew beards and moustaches but often kept their hair short at the back and sides. Owning a sword was a sign of wealth.

This is a reenactment of Vikings making swords.

TEXT-DEPENDENT QUESTIONS

1. What did the Swedish call Saturday?
2. What did Viking women and men wear?
3. What was considered a sign of wealth?

RESEARCH PROJECT

Many people think that a Viking helmet has horns. This is not true. A Viking helmet was more of a traditional medieval helmet. Do research about various medieval helmets, and create a visual presentation of the different styles you discovered in your search.

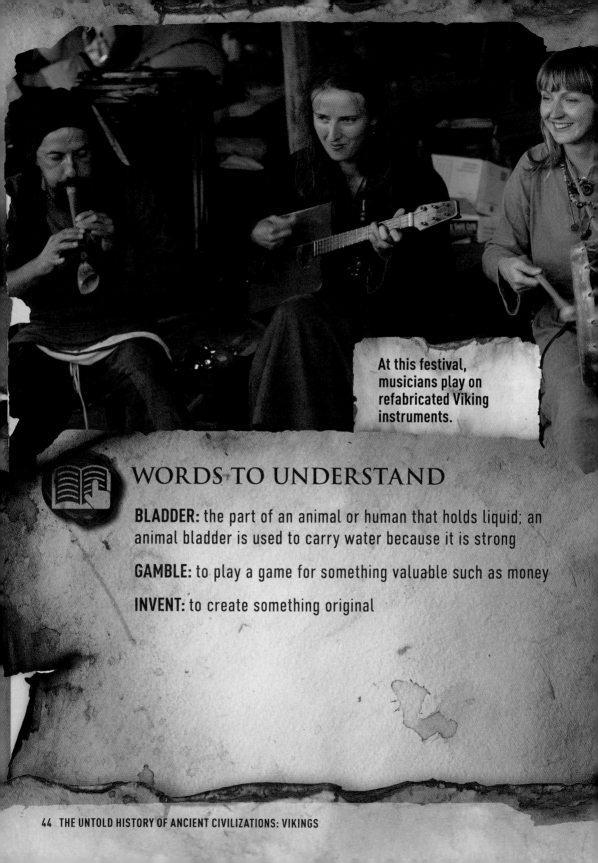

At this festival, musicians play on refabricated Viking instruments.

WORDS TO UNDERSTAND

BLADDER: the part of an animal or human that holds liquid; an animal bladder is used to carry water because it is strong

GAMBLE: to play a game for something valuable such as money

INVENT: to create something original

CHAPTER 9

WHAT DO YOU WANT TO PLAY?

When the nights got long and cold in the wintertime in the northern lands where the Vikings lived, they found themselves indoors around the fire—with no televisions, tablets, or even books!

They made their own entertainment, playing board games, telling stories, **inventing** poems and riddles, and singing songs. Viking songs were not to everyone's taste. Al-Tartushi, the Arab merchant who visited Denmark, wrote, "Nothing can compare with the horrible singing of these people. It's even worse than the barking of dogs!" None of the songs Vikings sang survive to today because no system for writing down music was invented until after the Viking age.

There were many different board games. The best known was called *hnefatafl,* or king's table. It was like a battle in which a king and his warriors were surrounded by a larger enemy army. The king, who began at the center, had to find a way through the enemy pieces and escape to the side of the board. You can find out how to play hnefatafl at the end of this chapter. Board game champions were held in high esteem as athletes.

Ancient Vikings
enjoyed horse fighting.

In Iceland and Norway, the most popular Viking sport was horse fighting. The sagas contain many stories of fighting pairs. Two stallions (male horses) were made to fight each other, while a crowd of onlookers **gambled** money on which horse would win. A good fighting horse was very valuable.

SOUND FAMILIAR?

When the sun shone, people played outdoor games, such as soccer with a blown-up pig's **bladder**. Men and boys enjoyed trials of strength and skill, including swimming, wrestling, or simply throwing large boulders. One game was like "Monkey in the Middle." Four people stood in a square, throwing a rolled-up bearskin to each other, while a fifth person tried to catch it.

The hnefatafl board game was a popular Viking pastime.

TEXT-DEPENDENT QUESTIONS

1. What did the Vikings do for entertainment?
2. What is another name for hnefatafl?
3. What was the most popular Viking sport?

RESEARCH PROJECT

PLAY HNEFATAFL

Why not make your own board and pieces for hnefatafl, the Viking board game? Use a piece of square card for the board, drawing straight lines across it, to divide it into seven rows of seven squares. Make the pieces from modeling clay. There should be nine white pieces, including one larger piece, the king, and 16 black pieces. Set the board up like the picture at the top of this page.

HOW TO PLAY

The players take turns, moving one piece at a time, with white moving first. A piece moves any number of squares in a straight line, up, down, or from side to side, like a rook in chess. A player captures an enemy piece by getting two pieces into squares on either side of it. The captured piece is removed from the board. Black wins by surrounding the king on four sides. White wins if he can get his king to one of the sides of the board.

For the Vikings, Odin was considered the king of the gods.

WORDS TO UNDERSTAND

ANGLO-SAXONS: the name of the Germanic people who invaded England in the fifth and sixth centuries and were living there at the time of the Norman Conquest

CHARIOT: a two-wheeled, horse-drawn vehicle that carried one person

COCKEREL: a young, domestic male chicken

CHAPTER 10

GODS WITH SUPERPOWERS

For the Vikings, Odin was the king of the gods—he was the god of war and magic. And he had his hands full keeping track of the other gods. Each of the gods had their own special powers, which the Vikings admired. If a Viking warrior was lucky enough, when his life ended, he would go to live in Valhalla, the home of the gods.

Like modern superheroes, each Viking god had his or her own special abilities and magic equipment. Freyr, the god of the Sun and crops, owned a magic ship called *Skidbladnir*. This was big enough to hold all the other gods yet could be folded up and carried in a little bag.

Thor was a red-bearded god who rode across the sky in a **chariot** pulled by two goats. He was armed with a mighty hammer called *Mjollnir* ("crusher"). Viking warriors wanted to be just like Thor. He was a friendly god, believed to bring good luck. On sea journeys, people asked Thor for good weather, and many Vikings gave their children names including "Thor," such as Thorvald, Thorbjorn, and

THANK THE VIKING GODS IT'S FRIDAY

Four days of the week are named after Viking gods: Tuesday (Ty's day), Wednesday (Odin's day), Thursday (Thor's day), and Friday (Frey's day). These were not named by Vikings but by the Anglo-Saxons, or English. Before they became Christians, the Anglo-Saxons worshipped the same gods as the Vikings.

Before battle Vikings would make sacrifices on altars, such as this one in Denmark.

Thora. Nobody was ever named after Odin, who was a much more frightening god and known as the father of all the gods.

Vikings won their gods' help by making sacrifices, or offerings, to them. Horses, dogs, goats, **cockerels**, and sometimes even people were killed as sacrifices.

This bronze sculpture shows Thor, the god of thunder with his hammer.

Their blood was offered to the gods, and their bodies were hung from trees or poles. Before a battle, Vikings sometimes promised the whole enemy army as a sacrifice to Odin. By doing this, they hoped that he would help them kill as many enemies as possible.

The Vikings soon discovered that most other Europeans were Christians. Many Vikings began to worship Christ while keeping their old beliefs. They might have thought it was better to be safe than sorry. Over time, the worship of the old gods died out. Yet people still enjoyed telling stories of the adventures of Thor and the other gods.

Many runestones are found with crosses on them, which might indicate a possible Christian influence from Europe.

TEXT-DEPENDENT QUESTIONS

1. Who was Odin?
2. What days of the week are named after Viking gods?
3. How did the Vikings get help from their gods?

RESEARCH PROJECT

Many cultures worship in different ways. What are some ways people worship? Compare these ways to the Viking gods and rituals.

This famous runestone from the 800s AD features the longest known runic inscription in stone.

WORDS TO UNDERSTAND

GRAFFITI: markings sketched on stone or some other surface

RUNES: Viking letters, designed for carving that were used on things like grave stones, swords, and jewelry

SKALD: a person who writes poems; a poet

CHAPTER 11

VIKING GRAFFITI

O din gave more to the Vikings than blessings—the Vikings believed he gave them **runes**, which are letters in a simple writing system. As a gift from the god, runes were thought to have special powers.

The Vikings had the idea that words make reality, and so runes were very powerful. Vikings sometimes used them in spells to try to make enemies fall ill or to help sick people get better. To heal a wound, a spell might be scratched on a piece of bone, which was wrapped in a bandage around the injury.

People also used runes for everyday purposes, such as writing their names on brooches or swords. Sometimes people simply wrote their names on walls. Viking names have been found scratched on statues and churches in Greece and inside

Take a virtual tour of the many runes found in Scandinavia.

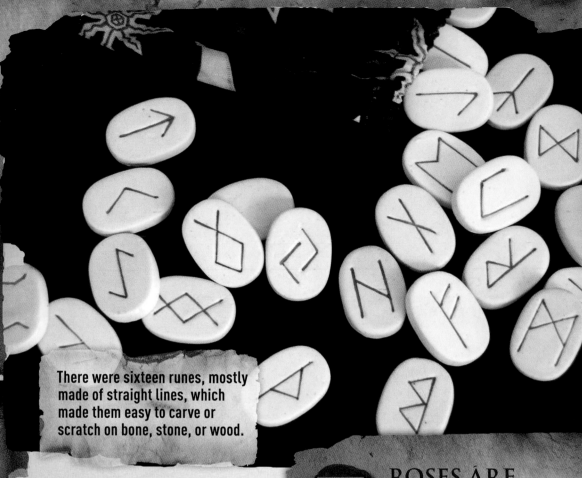

There were sixteen runes, mostly made of straight lines, which made them easy to carve or scratch on bone, stone, or wood.

ancient stone tombs in Orkney. Like **graffiti** writers today, Vikings liked leaving their names behind wherever they went.

In the Viking homelands, there are more than 3,000 standing stones carved with runes praising dead men and women, set up by their friends and relatives. Those for men say things like, "He was the terror of men and met his death in the East." Women were celebrated

ROSES ARE RED

In their poetry, Vikings liked to come up with unusual ways of describing everyday things. A ship could be called a "sea deer," a "wave horse," or a "sea bench." The sky might be "bird world," while the sea could be "whale home." Can you think of any other names for the sky and the sea?

You can see the individual letters on this runestone.

This runestone found in Sweden is a memorial.

for their skills running the house and farm. A typical stone says, "She was the most skillful girl in Hadeland." Every Viking man or woman hoped to be remembered well after death.

Another way of being remembered was in a poem. Viking rulers had their own **skalds** whose job was to invent poems praising their lord's generosity and bravery. Gunnlaug Snaketongue, Kormak Ogmundarson, and Hallfred the Troublesome Poet were a few of the more famous skalds in Iceland. Ordinary people also thought up poems to entertain their family and friends.

These standing stones, found in Sweden, were placed in the shape of a boat.

Vikings often made musical instruments from bull horns.

TEXT-DEPENDENT QUESTIONS

1. What did the Vikings use to write their language?
2. How many stone rune carvings been found at this point?
3. What job did the skalds have?

RESEARCH PROJECT

Watch to see rare Viking musical instruments and hear the sounds they made.

Not only did the Vikings carve runes on stone, but they also carved musical instruments. The video on this page discusses the different kinds of Viking instruments that have been found by archeologists. The video shows authentic Viking instruments, often carved out of wood, and demonstrates the kind of noise they make. Are these instruments similar to instruments you've seen before? Write a two- to three-page paper taking about the similarities between these Viking instruments and the instruments you know.

VIKING FACTS

The first Icelander *althing* (assembly) first met on this plain the year 930 AD.

VIKINGS TODAY: Although the Viking age ended almost 1,000 years ago, in some ways the Vikings are still with us today. Scientific tests have shown that many people living in the British Isles are descended from Viking settlers. In the Orkneys (islands off the northeast tip of Scotland), for example, more than three-quarters of the population is of Norwegian descent.

VIKING WORDS: In England, Viking settlers and English people lived side by side, and English speakers eventually picked up Scandinavian words. Hundreds of the everyday English words we still use are really Viking words. These include "happy," "law," "call," "take," "knife," "ugly," "fellow," "sky," "skin," "husband," "they," "window," and "anger."

YORKSHIRE SAYINGS: In places densely settled by Scandinavians, such as Yorkshire, there are even more Viking words. These include the Yorkshire greeting or warning "Hey up!" and words such as "gawp" (to stare at) and "dollop" (soft lump).

SCANDINAVIAN PLACES: If you look at a map of Britain, you will find hundreds of Scandinavian place names, telling us where Vikings once lived. The commonest end in "by," meaning homestead or village. But look out also for "thorpe" (new village), "holm" (island), "thwaite" (clearing), "wick"' (harbor), "dale" (valley), and "ness" (headland). Such place names often include the name of a Viking settler. Grimsby, for example, was a place where a Viking called Grim once had his homestead. Scunthorpe was the village of a Viking called Skuma.

FATHER'S NAME: In Iceland, people are even closer to their Viking past. Their language is much like that of the first Viking settlers, and they still use their father's first name as a surname, just as the Vikings did. For example, Gudrun the daughter of Erik would be called Gudrun Eriksdottir. Her brother Olaf would be called Olaf Erikson.

Every January, Shetlanders celebrate a fire festival where they burn a longship to remind them of their Viking past.

Grimsby in Britain is where a Viking called Grim had his homestead.

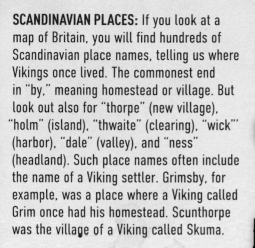

FURTHER READING

Gunderson, Jessica. *Vikings*. Mankato, MN: Creative Education, 2013.

Jeffrey, Gary. *The Dark Ages and the Vikings*. New York: Crabtree Publishing, 2014.

Lee, Adrienne. *Vikings*. North Mankato, MN: Capstone Press, 2014.

Stele, Philip. *Vikings*. Mankato, MN: Black Rabbit Books, 2014.

Woolf, Alex. *Meet the Vikings*. New York: Gareth Stevens Pub., 2015.

INTERNET RESOURCES

Surfing the Internet is the quickest way to find information about the Vikings. Here are some useful sites. Remember the Internet is constantly changing, so if you can't find these Web sites, try searching using the word "Vikings."

The Viking Network
http://www.viking.no/e/index.html

This Norwegian site, in English, is one of the best. It includes masses of information and project ideas, such as Viking recipes.

The Viking Answer Lady Webpage
http://www.vikinganswerlady.org/

Ask the Viking Lady to answer your questions!

History for Kids
http://www.historyforkids.org/learn/medieval/history/earlymiddle/vikings.htm

A description of Viking life with more sources to follow up with.

The Vikings for Kids and Teachers
http://worldhistory.mrdonn.org/vikings.html

Find interest facts and fun activities related to Vikings, plus use links to learn even more.

Translate Your Name in Runes
http://www.pbs.org/wgbh/nova/vikings/runesright.html

At the top of this page, you can type in your name, and it will show you how it would be written in Viking runes!

EDUCATIONAL VIDEO LINKS

Vikings 1: http://x-qr.net/1HpF
Viking Warfare experts talk about armor and gear worn by ancient Vikings.

Vikings 2: http://x-qr.net/1HVR
Explore the Vikings' world in this video from the National Museum of Denmark.

Vikings 3: http://x-qr.net/1Hnb
Watch as this video shows turf buildings in Iceland and Newfoundland.

Vikings 4: http://x-qr.net/1DMt
Take a virtual tour of the many runes found in Scandinavia.

Vikings 5: http://x-qr.net/1FsK
Watch to see rare Viking musical instruments and hear the sounds they made.

PHOTO CREDITS

INDEX

M

makeup, 42
medical care, 21
Mjollnir, 49
monestaries, 14–16
 see also religion
money, 31, 33 *fig*
monks, 14–15
 see also religion
music, 56 *fig*

N

names, 59
navigation, 25
Newfoundland, 28
nicknames, 8, 27
Norman Conquest, 48
North America, 25, 27
North Atlantic Ocean, 25
North Sea, 8 *fig*, 21, 25
Northumbria, 14
Norway, 7, 8 *fig*, 11, 31, 46
Norwegian Vikings, 8

O

Odin (god), 48–51, 53

P

parliament, 34
 see also politics
poetry, 6, 8, 45, 52, 54
 see also entertainment;
  storytelling
politics, 15, 34
professions, 7, 31

Q

QR Video
 runes, 53
 turf houses, 35
 Viking armor and gear, 19
 Viking instruments, 56 *fig*
 the Viking world, 7

R

Ragnar Hairy-Breeches, 19
raids, 6–8, 12 *fig*, 15–16, 40 *fig*
ravens, 27
religion, 11, 14–15, 48–51, 53
 see also spells
research project
 cardboard longship. *see* ships
 comparing worship customs, 51
 currency photo collage, 33 *fig*
 growing turf, 26
 playing *hnafatafl*, 47
 soap carving, 38 *fig*
 Viking helmets, 43
 Viking instruments, 56 *fig*
 Viking settlement map, 17
 Viking shield, 22, 23 *fig*
 writing with runes, 9
Rhine River, 20 *fig*, 21
riddles, 45
ring givers, 15
runes, 9, 52–54, 54 *fig*, 55
 see also writing
runestone, 51 *fig*–52 *fig*, 55
 see also runes
Russia, 8

S

sacrifices, 50–51
sagas, 8, 19, 25, 27, 46
Scotland, 36, 58
seabirds, 36
Seine River, 21
ships, 10 *fig*, 11–12
 decorations on, 11
 longships, 11
 see also longships
shrines, 14–15
 see also religion
singing
 see also storytelling
skald, 52, 55
 see also poetry

Skidbladnir, 49

slavery, 30, 32
soapstone, 35–36
spells, 53
 see also religion
sports, 46
standing stones, 54–56
storms, 16
storytelling, 45
sun stone, 25
Sweden, 7, 8 *fig*, 36
Swedish Vikings, 8, 41
swords, 43

T

thing, 34, 36–37, 58
 see also politics
Thor (god), 49–51
Thorstein Codbiter, 7
trade, 30 *fig*, 31–32
treasure, 16, 18, 21
Tryggvason, Olaf, 11
turf houses, 24, 27–28

U

Ulf the Unwashed, 7

V

Valhalla, 49
Vinland, 25

W

warships. *see* longships
weekdays, 49
writing, 6, 8–9
 see also runes